MW00803991

A Whaling Captain's Daughter:

The Diary of
Laura Jernegan, 1868–1871

Edited by Megan O'Hara,
foreword by Suzanne L. Bunkers

Content Consultant: Judy Downey, Librarian
New Bedford Whaling Museum,
New Bedford, Massachusetts

Blue Earth Books

an imprint of Capstone Press
Mankato, Minnesota

Blue Earth Books are published by Capstone Press
151 Good Counsel Drive, P.O. Box 669, Mankato, Minnesota 56002
http://www.capstone-press.com

Library of Congress Cataloging-in-Publication Data
Jernegan, Laura, b. 1862.
  A whaling captain's daughter: the diary of Laura Jernegan, 1868-1871 / edited by Megan
O'Hara : foreword by Suzanne Bunkers.
  p. cm.—(Diaries, letters, and memoirs)
  Includes bibliographical references (p. 31) and index.
  Summary: The diary of a young girl who traveled with her family on her father's whaling
ship from 1868-1871 records her schooling, dangerous whale hunts, and the processing of whale
oil. Includes sidebars, activities, and a timeline related to this era.
  ISBN 0-7368-0346-7
  1. Jernegan, Laura, b. 1862 Diaries—Juvenile literature. 2. Jernegan, Laura, b. 1862—
Journeys—Juvenile literature. 3. Girls Diaries—Juvenile literature. 4. Seafaring life—Juvenile
literature. 5. Whaling—Juvenile literature. [1. Jernegan, Laura, b. 1862. 2. Seafaring life.
3. Whaling. 4. Diaries. 5. Women Biography.] I. O'Hara, Megan. II. Title. III. Series
G545.J47 2000
910.4'5'092—dc21   99-15275
                                                                                CIP

Editorial credits
Editor: Kay M. Olson
Designer: Heather Kindseth
Illustrator: Linda Clavel
Photo researchers: Heidi Schoof
    and Katy Kudela
Artistic effects: Louise Sturm-McLaughlin

Photo credits
Martha's Vineyard Historical Society, 6, 8;
Archive Photos, 9; San Francisco Maritime
National Historical Park, 11, 20; Photri,
12; North Wind Picture Archives, 10, 13,
14, 19, 24, 28; Robert Weiss, 16;
Old Dartmouth Historical Society, 18.

CONTENTS

Editor's Note

The Diaries, Letters, and Memoirs series introduces real young people from different time periods in American history. Whenever possible, the diary entries in this book appear word for word as they were written in the young person's original diary. Because the diary appears in its original form, you will notice some misspellings and mistakes in grammar. To clarify the writer's meaning, corrections or explanations within a set of brackets sometimes follow the misspellings and mistakes.

This book contains only portions of Laura Jernegan's diary. Text has sometimes been removed from the individual diary entries. In these cases, you will notice three dots in a row, which are called ellipses. Ellipses show that words or sentences are missing from a text. In 1929, *The New England Quarterly* reprinted Laura Jernegan's diary, edited by Marcus Wilson Jernegan. A copy of this reprint is currently held in the collection of the New Bedford Whaling Museum.

FOREWORD

I started writing in a diary when I was 10 years old. At first, I wrote short entries about the weather, family activities, schoolwork, and friendship. I soon began to write about my thoughts and feelings. My hopes and dreams for the future eventually found their way into my diary. I have kept a diary for more than 35 years. Writing in it is still one of my favorite things to do.

Diaries like Laura Jernegan's and mine are called primary sources. Primary sources are letters, photographs, diaries, and other materials that give firsthand accounts of people's lives. We learn about personal views of history from primary sources. They detail the events and feelings people have experienced.

Today, primary sources such as Laura Jernegan's diary show us how people lived in the past. We learn about the challenges people have faced. We learn about their accomplishments. Their stories help us understand how past events have led to the present.

Suzanne L. Bunkers
Professor of English and
Director of Honors Program,
Minnesota State University, Mankato

Laura Jernegan
A WHALING CAPTAIN'S DAUGHTER

Laura Jernegan was the daughter of a whaling captain. In 1868, Laura Jernegan was 6 years old and her brother Prescott was 2 years old. Their father, Jared, and their mother, Helen, decided to bring the children on a five-month voyage aboard his bark, the *Roman*. This whaling ship was 100 feet (30 meters) long and included a crew of men who hunted whales, sewed and repaired sails, and guided the ship through rough and calm seas.

Laura traveled with her family on many ocean voyages. During the 1868 voyage, the family and crew sailed from New Bedford, Massachusetts. They traveled around the southern tip of South America and across the Pacific Ocean to the Hawaiian Islands.

Aboard the *Roman*, Laura's mother encouraged Laura to keep a diary. Laura faithfully kept her diary until she was 9 years old. She often recorded short entries, writing only what the family had to eat that day. Laura ended every day's entry with the words "Good Bye for To Day." Each of Laura's diary entries gives us a glimpse of what life was like aboard a whaling ship in the late 1860s.

Laura Jernegan wrote in her diary about life aboard a whaling ship.

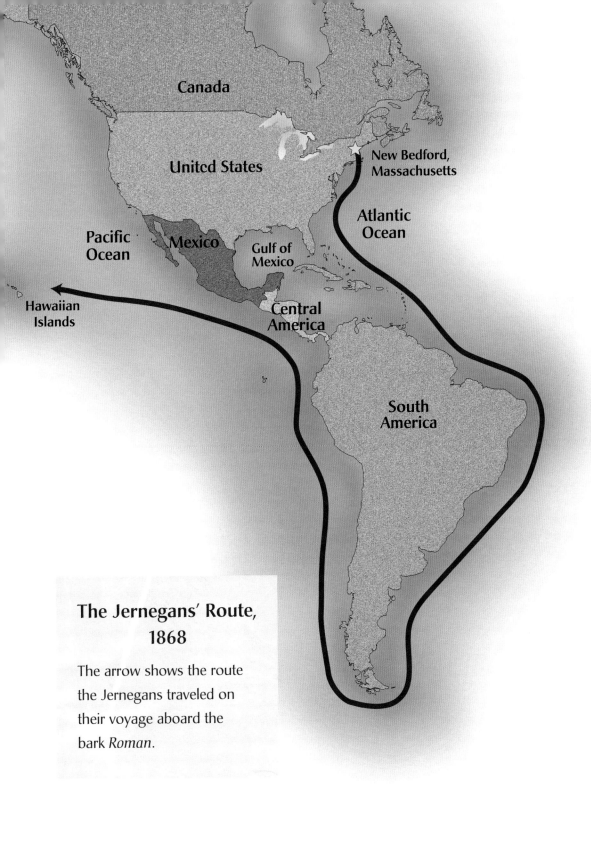

Canada

United States

Pacific
Ocean

Mexico

Gulf of
Mexico

Hawaiian
Islands

Central
America

Atlantic
Ocean

New Bedford,
Massachusetts

South
America

The Jernegans' Route, 1868

The arrow shows the route
the Jernegans traveled on
their voyage aboard the
bark *Roman*.

The Diary of Laura Jernegan

Dec. 1st 1868—

It is Sunday and a very pleasant day. I have read two story books. This is my journal. Good Bye For To Day.

Tuesday 14—

To day Papa is making a mark [flag] to show the men where the whles arer [whales are]

Barks and Whaleboats

A bark was a type of whaling ship. Barks were built for strength, not for speed. At about 125 feet (38 meters) long, these sturdy ships were designed for sea voyages of up to four years. A bark served as a factory for making whale oil and a place for storing the oil. The ship also had living space for the captain and crew. Barks usually carried four or five whaleboats. Whaleboats were smaller boats used to get close to a whale during a hunt. Whaleboats were about 30 feet (9 meters) long and 6 feet (2 meters) wide. Each whaleboat held a crew of six men.

This model of the bark Roman *is on display at the Martha's Vineyard Historical Society Museum, near the place where the actual bark set sail.*

Sperm Whales

For whalers in the 1800s, a sperm whale was a valuable catch. A large sperm whale had enough blubber to make 100 barrels of whale oil. Whalers could sell the high-quality oil made from the sperm whale's blubber for a good price. People used spermaceti from the head of sperm whales to fuel lanterns, to make candles, and to make face and hand creams.

Sperm whales are the largest of all toothed whales. Adult males measure 50 feet to 52 feet (15 meters to 16 meters) long and weigh up to 40 tons (36 metric tons). Adult females measure 33 feet to 36 feet (10 meters to 11 meters) long and weigh about 14 tons to 18 tons (13 metric tons to 16 metric tons).

Sperm whales breathe through an S-shaped blowhole in the center of their heads. This blowhole can shoot air up to 50 feet (15 meters), making a noise that can be heard up to one-half mile (.8 kilometers) away. After taking a breath through their blow holes, sperm whales can stay underwater for more than one hour.

Whalers respected sperm whales. Sperm whales put up a fight, thrashing and rolling in the water after being struck by a whaler's harpoon. A harpooned whale tried to escape by sounding or fleeing. When a whale sounds, it dives deep into the ocean and travels quickly. A fleeing sperm whale can swim more than 25 miles (40 kilometers) per hour.

Saturday 5th—

Papa spoke [to the crew of] the ship Annawan. Capt. Russel came on board of the Roman.

Monday 7th—

They have taken four sperm whales. It is nice fun to see them.

Wednesday 9th—

The men are boiling the blubber that makes the oil

Gales, Squalls, and Tempests

Whalers kept a constant watch on the weather. Weather on the ocean can change very quickly. Dangerous gales, squalls, and tempests can form suddenly with little warning. A gale is a strong wind. A squall is a sudden, strong wind that usually brings rain, snow, or sleet. A tempest is a violent storm.

The crew sometimes would mistake a tempest for a whale spouting off. A closer look would show a storm coming instead of a whale. Whaling crews hurried to take down the sails when a storm approached. Flying sails in strong winds was dangerous because a ship could easily be tossed below the waves.

Lady Ships

In the mid 1800s, some captains brought their wives and children aboard whaling ships to keep their families together during long voyages. Whalers sometimes called ships with women on board "lady ships." Some captains' wives would hold Bible classes for the crew, attend the sick and injured, or teach sailors how to read.

Saturday 12th—

We had a tempest last night and a squall this morning. Papa spoke [to] the ship Chnticleer [Chanticleer] and reported our oil. We have 60 barrels of sperm [whale] oil.

Sunday 13—

It is quite rough to day There is a ship in sight We have put on our flannels [warm underwear].

Thursday 15—

There is no wind to day. The men are stowing the oil down [below the deck] We have 4 ducks on board of our ship.

Friday 18—

The wind blows very hard. We had ducks for dinner. I study my lessons every day. Mama has given me some wosted [worsted wool yarn] and I am making a toilet cushion [seat pad for a stool or small bench].

Monday 4th January 1869—

We past by Cape Horn to day. It is a large black rock. Some of the rocks look like a steeple of a church.

Wednesday 6—

The men caught a goney [gooney bird] and we had it on deck.

Monday 11—

We have had a gale two days. It is now moderate. We had corn beans for dinner. I am geting along with my lessons nicely.

Friday 15—

We have been in sight of Tres Montes [in Chile]. It is a large mountain. The gonneys [gooney birds] have been flying around the ship.

Sunday 17—

Papa spoke [to] the ship Mornin Star [Morning Star] Capt. Allen came on bord of the ship Roman. Uncle Nathen came on bord of us at one oclock.

Monday 18—

Uncle Nathen came on bord and spent the forenoon. He gave us some sweet potatoes and some limejuice and some coconuts and a few pumpkins.

Tuesday 19—

Papa opened one of the coconuts. It is soft inside. Prescott loves them. Thare is a fly on my finger. He has flew of [off] now.

Monday 25—

This afternoon Papa and Mama went ashore of Juan Fernandes [an island in the South Pacific off the coast of Chile] She brought me a basket of flowers.

Gams

Whaling crews that were at sea for months and years became lonely. When whaling ships passed one another, the captains and crew members enjoyed visiting. These visits, called gams, gave the sailors a chance to share news from home.

Ships pulled alongside each other during gams. The captains talked back and forth with bullhorns, which they called speaking trumpets. A captain and crew sometimes would board the other ship for a longer gam. These visits might include music, dancing, and storytelling. The captains traded mail, newspapers, books, maps, and other materials.

Most gams were chance meetings with strangers. But Laura's father and her Uncle Nathan had planned their gam. These skilled seamen managed to meet at an appointed time and place in the middle of the ocean. The two brothers had not seen each other in four years. They were happy to exchange supplies and news of home.

Monday February 1st 1869—

It is a calm day and very pleasant. Papa has made two boat sails …

Wednesday 3—

It rained a little this moning. Papa is nailing boards on the deck. Prescott has got some nails and [is] pounding them in a board.

Thursday 4—

Mama is making a toilet cushion [a seat pad for a stool or bench]. It is made of red and green wosted [worsted wool yarn]. Papa has made Prescott a hat out of my shaker [sweater]. We have fair wind now. We had green peas for dinner.

Friday 5th—

It is a pleasant day and a fair wind. Papa saw diamond fish from the mast head. Prescott is out on deck.

Saturday 6th—

It is a warm day. I shall finish my third reader this afternoon. Papa is making a jib …

Monday 8—

It is a warm day and very pleasant. Mr. Wilber struct [struck] a fish this forenoon. The fish is albacore [tuna].

Tuesday, 9—

It is a pleasant day Papa saw some whales from the mast head.

Wednesday 10—

Papa has got two whales. Papa said that the men would boil out the bluber. There was a bird flew on board of the ship Roman

A Whale Hunt

Crew members took turns watching for whales. The lookout stood atop the masthead, 100 feet (30 meters) above the ship's deck. The lookout watched for a whale to surface for air. The whale breathed out a huge spout of misty water. The lookout cried, "There she blows!" when he spied a whale spout.

When the crew heard the lookout's call, they ran to stations on the whaling ship's deck. A bark had three to five small whaleboats strapped to the side of the ship. The crew climbed into the whaleboats, lowered the boats into the water, and followed the whale.

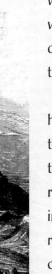

The harpooner stood at the front of the boat with his knee braced on a support. The harpooner aimed the 10-foot (3-meter) harpoon at a spot just behind the whale's head. When the boat was within arm's reach of the whale, the harpooner hurled his weapon into the whale. At that moment, the boatsteerer at the rear of the boat yelled, "Stern all." This order meant the oarsmen had to back the whaleboat away from the whale as fast as possible.

The harpoon used to spear the whale had about 1,800 feet (550 meters) of rope. A harpooned whale could swim for hours. The whale would gradually tire and float exhausted on the ocean's surface.

The boatsteerer was a whaler who made the final kill. He stabbed the whale with a razor-sharp lance. The whale would drown in its own blood, spouting blood instead of air and water. When blood spouted from the whale's blowhole, sailors said the whale had its "chimney afire."

Thursday 11—

The men have finished just boiling the oil. It is a very warm day. I have just commenced my geography. I like it much. We had green peas for dinner.

Friday 12—

They have taken forty teeth out of the largest sperm whale. The deck is very clean and white.

Scrimshaw

Whalers sometimes spent weeks at sea without spotting a whale. They made up hobbies to pass the time. One hobby was called scrimshaw. Scrimshaw was the art of scratching designs on teeth, bones, and other hard parts of animals. Using a jackknife, whalers might carve a scene of men killing a whale or a picture of their ship onto a whale's tooth. Whalers often used sperm whale teeth for scrimshaw. Sperm whale teeth could be up to 6 inches (15 centimeters) long.

Whalers spent many hours filing, sanding, and polishing the rough texture of the whale tooth. They scratched designs into the polished tooth surface. They then filled the scratches with ink to make the design show clearly. Whalers gave scrimshaw pieces to family members or sold them as art. Some sailors became good at carving scrimshaw designs onto useful items such as rolling pins, doorknobs, and walking canes.

Scrimshander Robert Weiss carved images of Laura's parents, Helen and Jared Jernegan, on fossilized walrus tusks.

Sunday 14—

It is very pleasant. Prescott is out on deck. Prescott is looking at the pictures. We have 4 chickenon [chickens on] board of our ship. We have six pigs on board. Papa is up to the mast head. Mr. Dougherty is hanging out his clothes.

Monday 15—

Prescott is out on deck. Papa is making a sail. Stuard [Steward] has given me six wine glasses.

Tuesday 16—

The men have killed one of the pigs. We have five now. It is fair wind. Prescott is out on deck.

Wednesday 17th—

It is a very pleasant day I have had my lessons perfect.

Thursday 18—

I have just finished a story book called Little Prudy. Papa saw some grampuses [a type of small whale].

Friday 19—

I have had my lessons perfect. I am doing sums in divisson. I think it is nice. Mama is making some new waists [shirts]. Papa is geting a latitude. The men have been geting out watter. Prescott is out on deck.

Sunday 21th—

Mama is reading a book. Prescott is swinging. Prescott is sitting in the chair. It is very pleasant. I have a green pencel and some paper. And a little kinfe [knife]. Prescott is out on deck.

Tuesday 9th—

We hhav 195 barrels of sperm oil. It is a pleasant day. There is a ship in sight. We are most to Honolulu. Prescott is out on deck …

Friday 14—

I have been out on deck. Prescott has his rope. I am out on deck. We have 4 barrels of oil. Papa is makeing a boat sail. He is going to have a boat.

Honolulu, September 1870
Monday 26—

it has blown real hard for two days. Prescott cut his foot last night it bleed. I am in Honolulu. it is a real pretty place. Mama is making a dress for me. Papa is up north where it is cold, he will come back pretty soon. I have two kittens here and one aboard the ship.

Bark Roman
[Friday] February 10ht 1871—

it is quit[e] rough to day. But is a fair wind. We have 135 barrels of oil. 60 of humpback and 75 of sperm. We had too [two] birds, there is one now. One died. There names were Dick and Lulu. Dick died. Lulu is going to. Prescott has got a little dog, its name is Tony. We have not seen a ship since we have left Honolulu. Prescott is playing with Papa. I am in the forth reder, and the fith righting book.

Whaling was hard work that held many dangers for the crew. But the barrels of oil that whalers brought to port sold at a good profit.

The Jernegans in Hawaii

The *Roman* arrived in Honolulu, Hawaii, in March of 1869, five months after leaving the harbor at New Bedford, Massachusetts. Mrs. Jernegan, Laura, and Prescott settled into a rented cottage in Honolulu. Captain Jernegan and his crew sailed to the Arctic Ocean, where they hunted whales for several months.

Laura's diary skips the rest of 1869 and most of 1870. Captain Jernegan returned from the Arctic Ocean in the fall of 1870. The Jernegans left Hawaii and spent the following winter sailing near the equator. The weather in this area is generally warm.

Saturday 11th—

Lulu died last night. It is quite smooth to day. It does not blow very hard to day. I am eight years old and Prescott is four. Prescott has just goon [gone] down below. It is most dinner time and I am very hungry. We are to have fresh mutton for dinner. Papa put up a hammock for Prescott and me. Mama is going to make a sack [dress] for herself. Papa is fixing the sink.

19

Children often had chores aboard whaling ships. This boy is feeding chickens to ensure a steady supply of eggs.

Sunday 12th—

it is Sunday. it rained last night. Papa made a trap and caught 5 mice, and mama has some hens that have laid 37 eggs. Prescott is out on deck. Prescott says that he has been out on deck and has only been talking to Cook and has been fixing his flag. it is not very pleasant to day. The man at the mast head first, siad he saw a whale. I hope we shale [shall] get him. it is most dinner time. we have had dinner. we had mutton for it.

Monday 13th—

it has rained all the morning and is very unpleasant. Papa has been fixing the sink and it runs real nice we have had dinner, we had corn for dinner, and we had baked potatoes for supper. The sun was out this afternoon. it has been calm all this afternoon, but rainy.

Tuesday 14th—

Mama has 44 eggs. We saw a ship her name was the lizzyrosy. Papa spoke [to] her. it is quite pleasant today, and smooth, we saw black fish this morning and Papa lowered the boats, they did not catch any we lowered the boats this afternoon but have not caught any yet but i hope we shal.

20

Wednesday, Feb. 15th 1871—

it is quite pleasant today we had sammon [salmon] for breakfast. it is quite cool today. we saw a ship today it was the Emmile Morgan [Emily Morgan] Mrs. Dexter came on board and we had a game [gam.] papa has just goon [gone] on board to get some papers. he is comeing back pretty soon. I will write some more.

Thursday 16th—

it is quite pleasant to day, the hens have laied 50 eggs. Papa came home last night and broght lots of papers and books. Mrs. Dexter sent Prescott and I some candy. Papa has a trap and has caught 6 mice. we caught one last night. The first one we caught was quite a large one. it is quite smooth to day. Prescott is up on deck playing. I am going up now to swing. Papa is fixing the water closet [toilet]. Prescott is eating eggs. he loves them. so do I. we had piecoe [pickles] for dinner. We are going aboard of the ship Emily Morgan to see some dogs. I think I shal have a good time. I went on board the Emile Morgan and had a nice time. Mrs. Dexter gave me some cards to play with, and a bottle of hair oil. and she gave me a little dog but we forgot him.

Friday 17th, 1871—

It is quite pleasand to day, it is quite rough to day. Papa is makeing a book-case. we had biskit [biscuits] for supper. I cant think of much to write. I have been swing[ing] to night, and prescott he loves to. I do to. The Longitude was 115-37. Papa is fixing the water closet…

Saturday 18th—

it has been quite rough this afternoon. I want to go to Honolulu very much. Prescott is up on deck playing. I am going up now. Prescott first came down hear [here] he did not speak to me. We saw a jumpper [fish]. Papa thougk [thought] it was a sperm whale, but it was not. Mama has 60 eggs.

Sunday 19th 1871—

it is quite pleasant today. I have not been on deck to day. Prescott has, he has just come down hear. I cant think of much to write. we had pancakes for supper. they were real good. it is most night. the Longitude was 117-23. I dont know what the Latitude was.

Latitude and Longitude

Globes and maps often have vertical and horizontal lines. The lines form an imaginary grid over the land and seas. The vertical lines on the grid are called longitude lines. The horizontal lines on the grid are called latitude lines. Sailors used the longitude and latitude lines to chart their location in the ocean.

Sailors figured latitude and longitude in degrees. The longitude lines run from the North Pole to the South Pole. The prime meridian is 0 degrees longitude and runs through Greenwich, England. The longitude is measured in degrees east or west of the prime meridian. The longitude number is followed by a letter W for West or E for East.

Latitude lines run horizontally parallel to the equator. The equator is at 0 degrees latitude. It is 90 degrees to the North Pole and 90 degrees to the South Pole. The latitude is measured in degrees north or south of the equator. For example, New Bedford, Massachusetts, is located at about 70°W longitude and 40°N latitude.

Look at this map. Find where you live. Between which two longitude lines is your home? Now find the nearest latitude lines. Between which two latitude lines is your home?

Arctic
Ocean

Greenland

90°N
80°N
70°N

60°N

Canada

50°N

United States

40°N

New Bedford,
Massachusetts

Pacific
Ocean

Atlantic
Ocean

30°N

New Bedford,
Massachusetts
70°W longitude
40°N latitude

Mexico

Gulf of
Mexico

20°N

0°W

110°W

100°W

90°W

80°W

70°W

Monday 20th 1871—

it is quite pleasant to day we saw whales this morning, we lowered the boats and we got six, the men are cutting them in now. Papa said the men would get 2 cut in to night but I think we shal only get one cut in. Prescott is up on deck seeing the men cut the whale in. the first Mate got 2 and the Second Mate got 2 and the third mate got too. I cant think of much to write. Mama is up in the house reading a book. I am going up on deck to see the men cut in the whale. Mama has 70 eggs. the men have got 2 whales cut in. it is most supper time …

Tuesday 21th 1871—

It is quite pleasant today. the men are cutting in the whales. they smel dredfully. we got a whale that made 75 barrels[.] the whales head made 20 barrels of oil. the whales head is as big as four whole rooms. and his boddy as long as one ship. the men have got 5 whales cut in, they have throne [thrown] some of the whale over board. it is fun to see them cut the whales in. Mama has just come doon [down] stairs, and Prescott I just went up on deck and the men were just geting the last pease [piece]. when they get done they all hury, hury, and five and forty More. Papa said that he would put some whales down in my journal, but I dont think so. Prescott is up on deck. I am going up on deck. the men have just began to boil out the blubber.

Wednesday 22th 1871—

it is a pleasant day, it is quite smooth to day. the men are boiling out the blubber in the try pots. the pots are real large. when the men are going to boil out the blubber, too [two] men get in the pots and squis [squeeze] out the blubber and are way up to there [their] knees of oil. when the men at the mast head say there she blows, Papa gives them 50 pounds of tobacco. Prescott is up on deck, and Mama too. I am going up too. it is most supper time. I have been up on deck. I cant think of muck [much] to write. I went to bed last night and got up this morning. we had baked potatoes for supeper [supper] and biscute [biscuit]. would you like to hear some news[?] well I dont know of any.

Making Whale Oil

The process of making oil began as soon as crew members tied a whale alongside the ship. The crew worked from a platform suspended above the whale. The crew cut into the whale's blubber with long-handled spades or knives. They removed the blubber in long strips that weighed about 1 ton (1 metric ton) each. The crew called these strips blanket pieces. Crew members hauled the blanket pieces onto the deck with a giant hook attached to a rope and pulley system.

Once the blubber was on deck, the crew prepared it for boiling. They cut the blanket pieces into smaller strips called horse pieces. They then cut the horse pieces into thinner slices. The skin looked like a book binding and the blubber looked like thick book pages. Whalers called these pieces Bible leaves.

Bible leaves were the right size to try out, or boil, in large try pots on the deck of the ship. Workers lit a wood fire in a brick furnace with a chimney stack called a tryworks. Huge 300-gallon to 400-gallon (1,136-liter to 1,514-liter) try pots held the cooking blubber. The blubber at the bottom of the pots shriveled first and forced out the oil. The oil slowly rose to the top of the pot. When all the blubber cooked away, only the oil was left. When the oil cooled, workers poured it into large barrels. They stored the barrels in the hold at the bottom of the ship. The ship's owner sold the oil after the ship returned to port.

Starting Your Own Diary

Laura kept her diary in part to help pass the long days at sea. She often mentioned the weather and family meals in her journal. She wrote about her parents' activities as well as what she and her brother did each day. All of these subjects are great topics for a journal. You can keep a journal to record your life and what is happening in the world each day.

What You Need

Paper: Use a blank book, a diary with a lock, or a notebook. Choose your favorite.

Pen: Choose a special pen or use different pens. You might want to use different colors to match your different moods.

Private time: Some people write before they fall asleep. Others write when they wake up. Be sure you have time to put down your thoughts without interruptions.

What You Do

1. Begin each entry in your diary with the day and date. This step helps you remember when things happened. You can go back and read about what you did a week ago, a month ago, or a year ago.
2. Write about anything that interests you. Write about what you did today. Describe people you saw, what you studied, and songs you heard.
3. Write about your feelings. Describe what makes you happy or sad. Give your opinions about things you see, hear, or read.
4. Write in your diary regularly.

Thursday 23th 1871—

It is quite pleasant today. the men are boiling out the blubber. Papa says there will be 120 barrels of oil. If there is 125 barrels of oil there will be 200 barrels of sperm oil. I am going up on deck. Prescott is up on deck and Mama. it is most supper time. I dont know what we are going to have

Friday 24th 1871—

the blubber is most all boiled out. Prescott is up on deck. We have had dinner, we had corn for dinner and beans. Mama is up on deck. I am going up.

Saturday 25th—

the men are putting the caskes [casks] down belowe. Prescott is up on deck it is most dinner time.

Monday 27th 1871—

it rained all this morning it has not been very pleasant to day, we are going to have corn for dinner and beans. P.S. it is quite rough to day.

Tuesday 28th 1871—

it is very rough today the men have got all through boiling the oil, they are whaseing [washing] of [off] deck. I am going up on deck.

Afterword

L aura grew up and married an officer in the Revenue Cutter Service, now called the U.S. Coast Guard. Later in her adult life, Laura made a sea voyage following the same route the *Roman* had traveled when she was a child. She wanted to see the scenes she remembered from childhood.

Laura's father was a whaling captain for 48 years and sailed on 16 ocean voyages. He died in January 1899. Laura's mother lived in a house on Martha's Vineyard until she died in in the 1930s.

Timeline

Congress approves the Homestead Act, which gives free family farms to settlers. Westward expansion begins.

The Confederacy surrenders, ending the Civil War (1861–1865).

| **1862** | **1865** | **1868** |

Laura Jernegan is born.

Laura begins her diary.

The Transcontinental Railroad is completed with a golden spike driven at Promontory, Utah.

Congress ratifies the 15th Amendment, giving African Americans the right to vote.

The Great Fire destroys Chicago.

1869   **1870**   **1871**

Captain Jernegan and his brother Captain Nathan Jernegan meet at an appointed spot in the ocean for a gam.

The Jernegans return to Honolulu. Captain Jernegan sails to the Arctic while his family stays in Hawaii.

The Jernegan family sails from Hawaii aboard the *Roman*.

Words to Know

cut in (KUHT IN)—to cut the layer of blubber from a whale's body

fleeing (FLEE-ing)—running away from danger

gooney bird (GOON-ee BURD)—an albatross, or sea bird, native to the Pacific Ocean

grampus (GRAM-puhss)—a small member of the whale family that often swims close to ships; the grampus makes unusual sounds like loud puffs or grunts.

harpoon (har-POON)–a long spear with an attached rope, usually used for hunting whales

jib (JIB)—a triangular sail in front of a ship's mast

mark (MARK)—a flag used by the ship's skipper to signal from the crow's nest to the men in smaller boats

mutton (MUHT-uhn)—meat from a sheep

parallel (PA-ruh-lel)—two straight lines that stay the same distance from each other and never cross or meet

rope and pulley (ROHP and PUL-ee)—a lifting device made from a rope and set of wheels with grooved rims

spermaceti (SPURM-uh-see-tee)—a substance found in the head of sperm whales that was used to make candles, lotions, and other materials

try out (TRYE OUT)—to boil whale blubber to extract the oil

try pot (TRYE POT)—huge pots used to boil whale blubber aboard whaling ships

tryworks (TRYE-wurks)—a brick furnace with a chimney stack to fuel fires under try pots

Internet Sites

In the Company of Whales
http://www.school.discovery.com/spring97/
programs/inthecompanyofwhales/vocab.html

The Kendall Whaling Museum
http://www.kwm.org

The Mariners' Museum
http://www.mariner.org

Mystic Seaport
http://www.mysticseaport.org

To Learn More

Gourley, Catherine, in association with Mystic Seaport Museum. *Hunting Neptune's Giants: True Stories of American Whaling.* Brookfield, Conn.: Millbrook Press, 1998.

Loeper, John J. *Meet the Allens in Whaling Days.* Early American Family. New York: Benchmark Books, 1999.

Murphy, Jim. *Gone A-Whaling.* New York: Clarion Books, 1998.

Ward, Nathalie. *Do Whales Ever…?* Camden, Maine: Down East Books, 1997.

Places to Write and Visit

Martha's Vineyard Historical Society
59 School Street
Box 827
Edgartown, MA 02539

Mystic Seaport
75 Greenmanville Avenue
P.O. Box 6000
Mystic, CT 06335-0990

New Bedford Whaling Museum
18 Johnny Cake Hill
New Bedford, MA 02740-6398

Vancouver Maritime Museum
Vanier Park
905 Ogden Avenue
Vancouver, BC V6J 1A3
Canada

INDEX